Couples Sma

BUILD YOUR MARRIAGE®

with

Couples of the Bible

by

Brad and Heidi Mitchell

Published by

Build Your Marriage

BuildYourMarriage.org

TABLE OF CONTENTS

INTRODUCTION

Build Your Marriage is a ministry committed to *helping couples build a Christ-centered marriage*. This study was written to draw couples closer to each other as a group as they work through each biblically-based topic. In addition, there are questions for you to discuss at home that will open conversation and understanding around each theme. Many couples have never prayed together, so there is a suggested prayer after sessions 2 – 9 based on each session's theme to help you get started.

You are encouraged to utilize the free resources offered by Build Your Marriage. At BuildYourMarriage.org there are articles addressing many issues faced in marriage. In addition, daily marriage encouragement is provided via social media on Facebook, Twitter, and Instagram.

Brad and Heidi Mitchell, the founders of Build Your Marriage, are available to speak at marriage conferences and retreats. Information about their speaking ministry can be found at the Build Your Marriage website along with contact information to check their availability.

It is our passion that you grow in Christ as you Build Your Marriage!

SESSION ONE

Build Your Marriage
by Knowing Your Group

Welcome to the Build Your Marriage small group study. We're so excited you've chosen to focus on the most important relationship in your life — your marriage. In this study, you'll be focusing on your marriage in a small group as you learn from couples in the Bible.

Each session begins with a "Getting to Know You" question, followed by an introduction of the biblical couple we will be studying each week. After the introduction, you'll read about the couple in the Bible and then have some questions to discuss in your small group. Choose as many (or as few) of these questions as you'd like. Then we suggest ending the evening with prayer.

There will be five questions at the end of each chapter to discuss on your own. You may choose to answer these questions all in one conversation or you may decide to answer one question each day for five days. Perhaps you'd like to discuss a question each day of the week, Monday through Friday. Whatever you choose is fine.

We do want to mention some guidelines for small groups. It's been our experience that small groups function best when these guidelines are followed:

1. Make sure everyone in the group has an opportunity to speak and share their thoughts. Don't monopolize the discussion.
2. What's said in the small group stays in small group. Confidentiality is vital.
3. Don't berate or criticize your spouse. This makes your spouse embarrassed and group members uncomfortable.
4. Focus on yourself when answering questions, not your spouse. Also, let each person tell their story; don't share it for them.
5. Be careful not to interrupt. Each group attendee deserves to be heard.
6. Refrain from gossip of *any* type.
7. Speak positively about your church and its leadership.

So let's get started!

Have each couple introduce themselves and tell one interesting fact about their marriage.

Next, have each couple tell how they met and what attracted them to their spouse. Give each couple 5-7 minutes to share their story.

Close the session with prayer requests and then pray for those requests.

SESSION TWO

Build Your Marriage by Trusting God

JOSEPH AND MARY

"Getting to Know You" Question

As a child was it easy for you to obey your parents or not? Why?

Overview of Joseph and Mary's Story

From the world's point of view, Joseph and Mary were the "least likely to succeed." They came from a small town called Nazareth. Scholars estimate the population was less than 500 at the time Jesus was born. Nazareth was an agricultural town growing grapes and olives. It was off the beaten path and had a poor reputation. When Nathanael, who became one of Jesus' disciples, heard that the Messiah had been found and he was from Nazareth he exclaimed, "Can anything good come out of Nazareth?" (John 1:46)

Joseph worked with his hands to earn a living as a carpenter. The average lifespan for an adult male was 40, and girls married young. Mary was most likely a young teen. They had an arranged marriage but hadn't yet had the ceremony. In their culture, being engaged (betrothed) was so binding that if a woman's fiancé died before they were married, she was still considered a widow. If you wanted to end the betrothal you had to get a certificate of divorce.

Although they lived about three days journey from Jerusalem (65 miles), they had a devout and uncomplicated trust in God. Their desire was to order their lives in such a way that they obeyed him and trusted him *no matter what the consequences might be.*

Even in the simple religious practices, Joseph and Mary were faithful. Forty days after the birth of their firstborn son, Joseph and Mary walked the six miles from Bethlehem, where they were living at the time, to the temple in Jerusalem. There, according to Jewish law they dedicated Jesus to God. The prescribed offering when presenting one's firstborn was a yearling lamb. But if a couple was too poor to present a lamb, they could give two pigeons. Joseph and Mary were so poor that was all they could afford.

As you study this passage, think about your choices as a couple. Where are you confident, or where have you been affirmed, that you have been making choices to be obedient and trust God? What are some areas the Holy Spirit may be nudging you to step out and trust God more? Is there anything for which the two of you need to ask God's forgiveness for *not* trusting him as you should have?

SMALL GROUP DISCUSSION QUESTIONS

1. In Matthew 1:18-25 the angel appears to Joseph, and in Luke 1:28-38 the angel appears to Mary. List your answers to these two questions below:

   What did the angel say to both Joseph and Mary that was the same?

   What things did the angel say to them that were different?

   Same   Different

2. What was Joseph's immediate reaction? What was Mary's?

3. Culturally, why would it have been hard for Joseph to obey God in this circumstance?

4. In Luke 1:38 Mary calls herself the "servant of the Lord." What do you think that meant for her?

5. How is it hard for you to obey God in our culture?

6. How can you be a "servant of the Lord" in your marriage?

7. When was a time you wish you had trusted God but didn't do so? What was the result?

8. What spiritual practices are present in your marriage that are acts of obedience to God?

9. Joseph and Mary dedicated Jesus to God. What are some of the things you and your spouse have dedicated to the Lord, either formally or informally?

10. Joseph and Mary had to sacrifice to give two pigeons at the temple. Describe a sacrifice that you and your spouse have made for God.

QUESTIONS FOR COUPLES AT HOME

1. Ask each other: Generally speaking, is it easy or hard for you to obey God? Why?

2. Share with your spouse an area where you are struggling to obey God.

3. In what area do we as a couple need to trust God?

4. Are there any spiritual practices we need to implement in our marriage?

5. Pray together as a couple asking God to help you trust him even when it's hard and you don't know the outcome. Commit yourselves to honoring God no matter what.

TO PRAY TOGETHER

Dear God,

We ask that you help us grow in trusting you in our marriage. We admit that it can be scary when we don't know the outcome. Help us to trust you one day at a time by taking the necessary steps of obedience. Please encourage us along the way.

In Jesus' name. Amen.

SESSION THREE

Build Your Marriage
by Influencing Your Spouse

AHAB AND JEZEBEL

"Getting to Know You" Question

Who, other than your spouse, has been the greatest influence in your life? How did this individual impact you?

Overview of Ahab and Jezebel's story

Ask for a volunteer to read 1 Kings 21:1-7, another to read verses 8-12, and another to read vv. 13-19.

Ahab was known as the most evil king to ever reign in Israel (1 Kings 21:25). He married the daughter of the king of Phoenicia, Jezebel. She was so evil that her name has become symbolic of false religion (see Revelation 2:20).

With his foreign wife, Ahab established worship of the false gods Baal (the storm god) and Asherah (the Canaanite goddess of fertility), as the official religion of Israel. The worship of Baal often included child sacrifice. Asherah worship involved all forms of sexual debauchery including ritual prostitution.

In 1 Kings 18 we are told that Jezebel sought to kill all of God's prophets in the land (vs. 4). Later in the same chapter, the prophet Elijah faced off against 450 prophets of Baal and 400 prophets of Asherah, with Ahab and others present. The challenge was to see whose deity would answer the call for fire from heaven. In the end, the 850 false prophets produced nothing. With one prayer from Elijah, though, God responded with fire from heaven on a clear day. As a result, all of Jezebel and Ahab's priests were killed… and Elijah went into hiding for a time.

Ahab ruled Israel for 22 years. His primary palace was in the capital city, Samaria, but he had a second palace constructed in Jezreel. Next to his palace in Jezreel was the home of a man named Naboth who owned a vineyard. Naboth's property would have been in his family for generations and would be passed on to his children and their children. (Jewish law was established to keep family property within the family.) Ahab's desire to purchase the property owned by Naboth ignored Jewish law and family property rights. Jezebel's actions to acquire the property were yet another example of her evil character.

Think about how you and your spouse influence each other. In what ways are you influencing each other toward good? How have you steered each other in paths that have led to hurtful places for yourselves or others? What steps can you take to be intentional toward a positive impact on one another?

1. Read 1 Kings 21:17-19 again. Why do you think the Lord said Ahab had murdered Naboth? (After all, Ahab never stoned Naboth.)

2. What does the word "influence" mean to you?

3. How did Jezebel misuse her power in her marriage to Ahab?

4. What is your opinion of Ahab? What are some better ways he could have responded to Jezebel?

5. When your spouse is upset because they didn't get something they want or thought they deserve, how do you respond? How does this help or hurt your marriage?

6. Revenge is defined in the dictionary as "the action of inflicting hurt or harm on someone for an injury or wrong suffered at their hands." (Dictionary.com) What are some ways couples commonly practice revenge toward our spouses and others?

7. Read Romans 12:14-19. Which of these commands did Ahab and Jezebel violate?

8. In a practical sense, how can you live out Romans 12:14-19 in your marriage? (Give specific examples, remembering not to criticize your spouse as you do.)

9. How has your spouse positively influenced you?

10. What is the biggest takeaway you have learned from Ahab and

Jezebel's marriage?

QUESTIONS FOR COUPLES AT HOME

1. Have we allowed the desire for revenge to creep into our marriage? How?

2. How have each of us positively influenced each other's spiritual journey?

3. How can we safeguard our marriage from bad decisions?

4. Has there been any misuse of power or authority in our marriage? What can we do to change it?

5. As a couple, pray together asking God to be the biggest influencer in your marriage. Repent together and ask for the Lord's forgiveness if there has been a pattern of revenge or misplaced authority in your marriage.

TO PRAY TOGETHER

Dear God,

We know that as a husband and wife you have given us the ability to influence each other. Our desire is to use that influence to draw us closer to you and each other. Forgive us for the times we have misused our authority in marriage or when we have sought revenge towards each other for _____. We don't want to do that anymore and we repent of the sin of revenge. Please grow us in your grace and help us to forgive each other quickly. We pray that our home will be one that is peaceful and unified and reflects your presence.

In Jesus' name. Amen

SESSION FOUR

Build Your Marriage
by Protecting Each Other Spiritually

ADAM AND EVE

"Getting to Know You Question"

Describe a time in your life when you felt protected by someone. Who was that person and how did they protect you?

Overview of Adam and Eve's story

Ask for volunteers to read Genesis 2:7-8, 15-18, 21-25, 3:1-13

On the sixth and final day of creation, God created the land animals and the man Adam. He placed Adam in the Garden of Eden to care for it. One of Adam's initial functions was to name each of the animals and birds. He had free rein over the entire garden with one exception, and the instructions were clear what he could and could not do (see vv. 16-17).

Knowing that Adam needed a companion, God created Eve as a "helper" for him. The connotation of her being a helper isn't a negative term. In fact, the same term is used of God being a help to us (cf. Psalms 33:20; 70:5; 115:9).

The Bible says Eve was formed by God from one of Adam's ribs. When God presented her to Adam, Adam recognized the unity they shared, declaring she was "bone of my bones and flesh of my flesh." Their relationship as the first husband and wife was so intimate, they were considered as "one flesh." The marriage of Adam and Eve was the completion of creation.

At some point during the days of creation one of the highest angelic beings, Lucifer (Satan), rebelled against God and was cast out of heaven. In Genesis he is present in the Garden of Eden. Lucifer has his first encounter with the man and woman who had been created in God's image. (Some scholars liken the description of the fall of the king of Babylon in Isaiah 14:12ff with the fall of Lucifer from heaven.)

It was there, at the beginning of creation, that Satan began his attack on marriage. His attack on marriage really represented his attack on

God. Satan didn't want people to reflect God's image or glory then, and he is even more fervent in opposition now (see Revelation 12:12b). Sadly, neither Adam nor Eve withstood his evil cunning, and the consequences of their sin have cascaded through history.

As you study this passage, be mindful of the attacks of the enemy on your own marriage. Where have you experienced his subtle lies? Where have you protected each other and stood strong? Where have you fallen prey to his attack? Resolve together that you will be unified in Christ as you take your stand against the devil's schemes (cf. Ephesians 6:13).

SMALL GROUP DISCUSSION QUESTIONS

1. Genesis 2:18 says, "It is not good that man should be alone." Why do you think God said that? Why would God have said that when everything else was good (and there wasn't even any sin in the world)?

2. Read Genesis 3:1 and notice the serpent's use of the phrase "Did God actually say...?" Satan tries to get us to doubt God in much the same way today. When in your life have you been tempted to compromise a godly conviction or command by doubting God's word(s) to you? How did you handle the situation?

3. Compare God's command to Adam in Genesis 2:15-17 with what Eve says to the serpent in Genesis 3:2-3. What instructions did Eve add to God's command? Why is this dangerous?

4. If we add or subtract details when communicating with our spouse, we can misrepresent facts to them. What are some common ways couples do this in marriage? Why do you think people do this?

5. Do you feel that Adam and Eve had wrong desires in eating the fruit? Why or why not?

6. Why do you believe the serpent went to Eve instead of to Adam?

7. In Genesis 3:6 Eve looks at the fruit. What three things does she notice about the fruit that led her to eat it? (Notice that none of these qualities were repulsive or bad in and of themselves.) How in our marriages are we tempted to trust what we see rather than what God has commanded us? Has there ever been a time in your marriage when you disobeyed the Lord, because you thought you knew better because of what you'd seen or heard?

8. Read Genesis 3:12-13. Isn't it interesting that Adam blames Eve for his eating the fruit and Eve blames the serpent for deceiving her? How could Adam and Eve have protected each other?

9. In marriage, we all are tempted to blame our spouse for situations that don't go well or for mistakes that are painful. Brainstorm as a group how you can constructively handle the temptation to blame your spouse.

10. What are the best ways you can protect your spouse spiritually? Use specific examples. What changes would you have to make in your marriage to implement these?

QUESTIONS FOR COUPLES AT HOME

1. Is there any area of our marriage where we are trying to hide something from God?

2. How does our companionship in marriage make us stronger?

3. How can we encourage each other when God's ways don't make sense, or when following his commands doesn't seem like a big deal?

4. As a couple, sit silently before the Lord for 2-3 minutes. Ask the Holy Spirit to reveal to you any area in your marriage where you have not protected your spouse spiritually. Then share with your spouse a step you will implement to protect your spouse spiritually.

5. Pray that in your marriage you will not blame or accuse each other. Pray that each of you can own your mistakes and sins and repent of those. Pray for protection from the enemy upon your marriage.

TO PRAY TOGETHER

Dear God,

We know that there have been occasions in our marriage where we have not wanted to accept responsibility for our wrongs. Instead, I, (your name)_____, have wanted to blame_____(spouse's name) for our difficulties, mistakes or sins. I ask your forgiveness for doing that. Help me to take full responsibility and ownership for my sins. I pray that I will protect _____(spouse's name)_____ spiritually by _____. Unite us spiritually by protecting each other and following you wholeheartedly.

In Jesus' name. Amen

SESSION FIVE

Build Your Marriage
with Sexual Purity

DAVID AND BATHSHEBA

"Getting to Know You" Question

When you think of the word "purity," what comes to mind and why?

Overview of David and Bathsheba's Story

They are one of the best-known couples in history. It's from their lives that we draw powerful insights into the importance of sexual purity in marriage. These two serve as a warning of what *not* to do. And they serve as a beacon of hope for those who have succumbed to sexual temptation of any kind.

Eventually they married, but their relationship didn't start that way. Instead, it began out of lust and passion. Their names are David and Bathsheba.

David had been king of Israel for over 20 years, and was now around 50 years old. He was the least likely to have been chosen king since he was the youngest of his brothers. He was a shepherd who had a heart after God. He trusted God when he faced and killed the mammoth giant, Goliath. He was skilled at writing songs of praise to God, and in fact wrote most of the Psalms. David was a valiant warrior and blessed by God with success as a leader.

We're told in 2 Samuel 5 that David became "greater and greater" because God was with him (vs. 10). And David knew it (vs. 12). It was in this season of success and seeming invincibility that David began making compromises in his sexual purity. While he didn't make alliances with foreign kings by taking their daughters as his wives, he *did* build his harem by taking wives and concubines from his own people (vs. 13). His sexual appetite went unchecked.

By the time we get to 2 Samuel 11, David was allowing himself more liberties as a result of his blessed success. It was the springtime when roads would be dry and troops with chariots could move freely into battle. Kings would travel with their troops and be with their men. But

David felt entitled to give himself a pass and stay at the palace. It was easier to delegate his responsibilities to his commander, Joab.

It is in this indulged and entitled state that we find David peering over his rooftop and watching Bathsheba bathe. She was alone at home because her husband, Uriah, was away with the troops. We're told in 2 Samuel 23:39 that her husband was one of David's top soldiers — a man of integrity and valor.

It's important to note that for all the sexual sin and consequences faced, David and Bathsheba stayed united until his death at an old age. Their second son, Solomon, succeeded his father as king. Solomon was known as the wisest man who ever lived and wrote much of the book of Proverbs. He was also the one charged by God to construct the temple in Jerusalem.

As you read the story of David and Bathsheba, be thinking about your own marriage and your standards for sexual purity. Is this something the two of you have talked about? Have you set up guidelines to protect yourselves? If you have suffered from any kind of sexual impurity, how have you brought God's grace and restoration into your relationship?

SMALL GROUP DISCUSSION QUESTIONS

1. Read 2 Samuel 10:17-19 and 2 Samuel 11:1-4. Is David at a low point or high point in his life when he initiates contact with Bathsheba? Is this surprising to you? Why or why not?

2. Every sin begins with a thought that is then acted upon. What was the progression of David's sin with Bathsheba? What do you think about the speed with which he sinned?

3. Read the phrase, "and David sent and inquired about the woman," and then consider our culture today. How easy is it to contact or connect with people? What boundaries do we as husbands and wives need to have in place if we try to reconnect with former co-workers or high school friends? Is it wise to do that? What are your thoughts? What standards for this, if any, do you have in your marriage?

4. Read 2 Samuel 12:1-14. What are all the consequences David will face for his sin? Who else has been affected by David and Bathsheba's sin? What happened to these people?

5. Look again at 2 Samuel 12:1-6. Nathan gives a word picture describing David's sin. Why do you think we can be hard on others who have committed similar sins and yet not see it in ourselves?

6. Consider if you were to engage in sexual sin. Who would be impacted by your sin? What could be some of the consequences for you and your spouse?

7. In 2 Samuel 12:13 David tells Nathan, "I have sinned against the Lord." In Psalm 51, written by David after his sin with Bathsheba, he says "For I know my transgressions, and my sin is ever before me. Against you, you only, have I sinned and done what is evil in your sight..." (vs. 3-4a). In these verses David recognizes that his sin doesn't just affect Bathsheba and himself. Rather, the impact of his sin is much larger — David has sinned against God! How should that perspective put a check in one's spirit when considering sexual temptation?

8. Romans 4:7-8 says, "Blessed are those whose lawless deeds are forgiven, and whose sins are covered. Blessed is the man against whom the Lord will not count his sin." Consider these words by David, the *former* adulterer, and the *former* murderer. How do these words give hope regardless of the sin that has been committed?

9. How can couples protect their marriage from sexual temptation?

10. What's one takeaway from this lesson that you'll apply to your marriage?

QUESTIONS FOR COUPLES AT HOME

1. Is there any area of our marriage where we have allowed sexual impurity? What are we going to do to change that?

2. Are we satisfied with the boundaries we have in place towards members of the opposite sex? Why or why not?

3. Do we demonstrate purity to each other and our family by the choice of movies, books, and TV programs that we watch? Does anything need to be eliminated?

4. What are the benefits for us of having a sexually pure marriage?

5. Spend time in prayer asking the Lord to bless your marriage with purity.

TO PRAY TOGETHER

Dear God,

Thank you for uniting us in marriage. As we reflect on sexual purity we repent of any areas where our marriage has not been pure. Help us to eliminate any desires that are not from you. Guard our hearts and our minds in Christ Jesus.

We ask that our marriage would be sexually pure and fulfilling from this day forward. We pray that we will recognize sexual temptation and flee from it. Protect our marriage from infidelity, lust, pornography, wrong desires, and other sexual sins. We want to honor you with our bodies and our marriage.

In Jesus' name. Amen.

SESSION SIX

Build Your Marriage
by Respecting In-Laws

MOSES AND ZIPPORAH

"Getting to Know You" Question

What is one character quality of your in-laws that you appreciate? (Please give an answer to this question even if your in-laws have passed away.)

Overview of Moses and Zipporah's Story

For the first 40-plus years of Moses' life he was single. Although he was a Jew, he had been raised in the home of Pharaoh in Egypt. But when he saw an Egyptian beating a Hebrew, he killed the Egyptian and ultimately went on the run for his life into the land of Midian located in the Sinai Peninsula.

The Midianites were distant relatives of the Israelites, having descended from Abraham through his wife Keturah (cf. Gen. 25:1-2). While sitting by a well, Moses watched as seven sisters came and drew water and filled troughs for their flocks. Then he saw some shepherds drive the women away from the troughs they had just filled. At that moment, Moses rescued the women so they could finish watering their sheep.

They introduced their hero to their father, Reuel (also known as Jethro), who was a priest of Midian. Jethro gave Moses his daughter, Zipporah, as his wife. They had two sons, Gershom and Eliezer.

There's no mention in the Bible of Jethro's wife. Most likely he was a widower raising his seven daughters alone. Moses worked for his father-in-law for 40 years tending his sheep in the desert. Looking at their long-term mutual respect and support, it can be inferred that they had a very good relationship.

When God directed Moses to return to Egypt, his father-in-law gave his blessing. Moses and Zipporah went to Egypt together. At some point, perhaps for her safety, Moses sent Zipporah and their sons back to Midian to be with Jethro. Moses clearly respected and trusted Jethro.

By the time Jethro and Moses were reunited, the ten plagues had been inflicted on the Egyptians, the Israelites had gone through the Red Sea, and God was providing manna for the Israelites to eat along with water miraculously spewing from a rock. The Israelites had just defended themselves against an attack by the Amalekites when Jethro arrived with Zipporah and their two sons.

Take a moment and read Exodus 18:7-10. The honor, respect, and relationship enjoyed by these two men is evident. Moses bowed to Jethro, kissed him, they inquired of each other's welfare, Jethro listened as Moses talked and then rejoiced at all the blessing Moses had experienced. Later on, as we will see, Jethro offers Moses some unsolicited advice.

As you discuss how to respect in-laws, keep in mind that doing what is right may not always be easy, convenient, or even seem just. There may be elements of sacrifice and grace that you will have to extend. Make the decision together to show mutual respect and honor to each other's parents.

SMALL GROUP DISCUSSION QUESTIONS

1. Exodus 2:15-21 gives us insight into the type of man Moses was. What do we learn about him from this passage?

2. Look at Exodus 2:15-21 again and also read Exodus 18. In what ways was Jethro (also known as Reuel) a good father and father-in-law? Give specific examples.

3. How does Moses honor Jethro?

4. What are some practical ways we can show honor and respect to our in-laws? What if your in-laws have lived in such a way that you don't think they're worthy of respect? Can you still show them honor?

5. Read Romans 12:13-18. How did Moses and Jethro live out this passage with each other? How can we apply this scripture to our relationship with our in-laws today?

6. In Exodus 18:13-17 we see Moses acting as a judge. What does Jethro say to Moses? Prior to that, we see Jethro asking Moses some questions. What are they? Jethro is seeking clarification and understanding before he determines what's in the best interest of the Israelites and Moses. Why is it important for husbands and wives to listen and understand before we offer advice or opinions to our spouse?

7. Jethro offers a solution to Moses. What is it? It's important to observe that Moses never asked Jethro for advice. Jethro offered unsolicited advice to his son-in-law. Why do you think Moses responded so favorably? What can we learn from this example?

8. Sometimes we may face burnout or get tired. Where in your marriage do you feel like you're carrying a big load? Brainstorm as a group how couples can accomplish their work and still protect each other from burnout. How have you been successful in your marriage in this area?

9. Jethro and Moses had a good relationship. If you don't like your in-laws or if they're different from you, do you still need to spend time with them? Why or why not?

10. What action step can you take to build a better relationship with your in-laws? Or if your in-laws are no longer living, how can you be a better mother-in-law or father-in-law to your son or daughter's spouse?

QUESTIONS FOR COUPLES AT HOME

1. What positive traits of our parents would we like to incorporate into our marriage?

2. How will we respond as a couple when we don't agree with the advice our parents or in-laws are giving us?

3. How can we show our parents honor? (If your parents are no longer living, ask yourselves "How can we be better in-laws to our son(s)- or daughter(s)-in-law?")

4. Is there an area of our marriage where we are over-extended? If so, how can we work together to share the responsibilities? What can we change?

5. Pray for your relationship(s) with your in-laws, daughter(s)-in-law, and son(s)-in-law.

TO PRAY TOGETHER

Dear God,

Thank you for bringing our family together. You designed each person and their habits and characteristics. You know our strengths and our weaknesses. Give us wisdom and grace as we try to honor <u>(parents' names, names of in-laws)</u>. Show us areas where we could strengthen that relationship. Give us the courage to step forward and do what's right and honoring.

We thank you as well for <u>(names of daughter(s)-in-law, son(s)-in-law)</u> who have married into our family. We ask that we would be prudent, loving in-laws and offer advice only after we listen and understand. Help us to control our words and be attentive to your Holy Spirit in our lives. We pray for a solid Christian family that honors every member with a Christ-like love.

In Jesus' name. Amen.

SESSION SEVEN

Build Your Marriage
with Good Stewardship

ANANIAS AND SAPPHIRA

"Getting to Know You" Question

What's a purchase you've regretted? Why?

Overview of Ananias and Sapphira's story

After Jesus' resurrection and ascension to heaven, the number of Christians multiplied in Jerusalem by the thousands. The unity they experienced was evident in the way they experienced community. Christians were gathering in each other's homes for meals, for mutual encouragement, and to meet one another's needs in tangible ways. There were healings taking place along with other signs and miracles that testified to the presence and power of Jesus Christ.

The unity among the Christ-followers was a testimony of Jesus' presence in their lives. Acts 4:32-37 describes how they were so connected in heart and soul that no one claimed personal ownership of anything. Instead, if there was a need, they would sell personal property to provide for the needs of others. The generosity and sharing were so great that for a while there wasn't anyone who had a need. The account in Acts gives the impression that there was almost a line of people selling their property and bringing all the proceeds to the apostles to distribute among the needy.

Ananias and Sapphira were among the new Christians who were also land owners. They had the means to sell property and still be financially viable.

We will see in this passage that they conspired together to appear more generous than they really were. When they sold a piece of property, it was Ananias who brought the money from the sale and presented it to the apostles. Sapphira didn't arrive until three hours later. And when Ananias gave the money, he presented it as though it was the full amount — and he was caught.

Through Ananias and Sapphira we see the high call that God has on couples to be united in generosity and honesty. As you talk about their lives, be open to God affirming you in your generosity. Pay attention to any nudges from him revealing places where the two of you need to grow in generosity and integrity.

SMALL GROUP DISCUSSION QUESTIONS

1. When in your life did you want to make a good impression on others?

2. Read Acts 5:1-11. What sins were Ananias and Sapphira guilty of committing? List them.

3. Look at Acts 5:4. Would it have been alright for Ananias and Sapphira to sell the land and keep the money for themselves? Why do you think they didn't do that?

4. When Peter says to Ananias that he chose to, "lie to the Holy Spirit" (v.3) and "You have not lied to man but to God" (v. 4), what do you think Peter means? How does lying to God differ from lying to men?

5. Why do you think the punishment for Ananias and Sapphira was so sudden and severe?

6. Have you exaggerated or misrepresented yourself to your spouse or someone else? How? What was the outcome?

7. How can we "test the Spirit of the Lord?" What does that mean (v. 9)?

8. Read 1 Peter 2:21-22. How can we as husbands and wives emulate Jesus and keep ourselves free from projecting a false image, or saying things that are untrue?

9. Look up the following verses: 2 Corinthians 9:7, Matthew 6:3-4, Matthew 6:19-21, Romans 13:7, Hebrews 13:5, 1 Timothy 6:17-19, and Proverbs 13:11. Which of these principles is the most difficult for you to practice in your marriage? Why? For you and your spouse, which are easier to implement?

10. Galatians 6:7 says, "Do not be deceived. God is not mocked. For whatever one sows, that will he also reap." How does this verse apply to Ananias and Sapphira's marriage? How does it apply to your marriage? What things would you like to "sow" in your marriage? Share them with your small group.

QUESTIONS FOR COUPLES AT HOME

1. Have we been good stewards of what the Lord has given us? Why or why not?

2. Is there anything we are lying about or misrepresenting to ourselves, our children, others, or God? How can we make it right?

3. Discuss what you would like to "sow" in your marriage. What steps can you take together to ensure this happens? Talk about how you can support each other to attain this.

4. Are we satisfied with the amount of money we give to the Lord? Why or not? How could we stretch our generosity as a couple in the area of money?

5. Pray together as a couple regarding stewardship, integrity, and money.

TO PRAY TOGETHER

Dear God,

Thank you for providing for us. We know that every good and perfect gift comes from you. You supply us with our needs and take care of us. We are grateful to you for blessing us with _____ (list things for which you're thankful) .

We pray that we will have integrity in the area of money. Help us not to misrepresent who we are or what we have to others. We pray for a heart of generosity and compassion towards others who are in need. Forgive us for the times where we have wasted money or been stingy. We surrender our finances to you. Please give us wisdom, unity, and clarity of purpose as we are stewards of your gifts to us.

In Jesus' name. Amen.

SESSION EIGHT

Build Your Marriage

through Pain

ZECHARIAH AND ELIZABETH

"Getting to Know You" Question

What's the most physical pain you've ever experienced in your life? When was this?

Overview of Zechariah and Elizabeth's story

Every marriage begins with hopes, dreams, and expectations: Who do you think our children will look like? What kind of parents will we be? Where do you think our careers will take us?

No matter what generation of history you look at, you'll find only slight variations on the same themes. The same was true for Zechariah and Elizabeth. In their culture, marriages were arranged. Girls married in their early to mid-teens. The average lifespan for men was only four decades, but Zechariah and Elizabeth had far surpassed that window. It's assumed that they were now in their 60s. The dream of having children of their own had long since passed.

Not only had they gone through the grieving, frustration, and pain of not bearing children, there was a social stigma in their culture that accompanied the inability to have children. It was believed that childlessness was a sign of God's judgment on a couple — especially the woman. In Luke 1:25 Elizabeth states that she had been under "reproach" (or disgrace) for her barrenness.

But Zechariah and Elizabeth are described as righteous and God-honoring. Each of them came from the priestly lineage of the Jewish tribe of Levites. That heritage would have indicated that they were doubly-blessed. But it didn't feel that way to them.

Everything started to change when Zechariah went to the temple to perform his priestly duties. The priests served on a rotating basis, each about twice a year, at the temple. When there, they would go through a selection process to choose one priest who would be privileged to enter the temple to tend the oil lamps, incense, and shewbread, and offer prayers on behalf of the people. While the priest was in the Holy Place of the temple, all the others would be outside on their faces in prayer until he emerged. This was a once-in-a-lifetime experience for a priest. Many priests would live their entire lives never getting that opportunity. But by God's design and timing, Zechariah's name was finally chosen.

Through their years of childlessness and sadness, Zechariah and Elizabeth had nurtured their relationship with tenderness and respect. As is evident by the story, they continued to be sexually intimate. When Elizabeth went into five months of self-imposed seclusion, it can be inferred that Zechariah took care of her. At the point of their son's birth, Elizabeth respected what Zechariah had been told about the name of their son, even amidst community pressure to name him otherwise.

Learn from Zechariah and Elizabeth how to stay tender and unified in the painful seasons of life. Observe their steadfast commitment to honor God throughout their lives. Renew your decision that you will "for better for worse, richer or poorer, in sickness and in health, love, cherish, and serve, for as long as we both shall live."

SMALL GROUP DISCUSSION QUESTIONS

1. Read Luke 1:5-25. What do we learn about Zechariah and Elizabeth? What kind of people were they? What had Zechariah been praying for?

2. Despite a long marriage, Zechariah and Elizabeth experienced pain in their life as a couple. Why? What are some other ways couples can have pain in marriage?

3. Turn to your spouse. Together agree on a painful experience in your lives that you can share with the group.

4. Gabriel says to Zechariah in vs. 13, "your prayer has been heard." When in your marriage have you prayed for something and finally, after many years, God answered your prayer? What were you praying for?

5. If the Lord doesn't answer your prayers the way you would like, how are you tempted to respond? What did Zechariah and Elizabeth do?

6. Elizabeth recognizes that God has shown her favor (v. 25). What are some ways God has blessed your marriage by showing you and your spouse favor?

7. When Zechariah and Elizabeth have their son, John, others rejoice with them. How can we support others in their pain and how can we share in their joy? Share some tangible examples.

8. Read Luke 1:57-66. What does Zechariah do as soon as he can speak (v. 64)? How can praising God help us as we are experiencing pain? (We don't praise God FOR the pain. We praise him despite the pain - IN the pain.) Why is it good to praise God when the pain is gone?

9. How can we stay tender toward our spouse through the highs and lows of marriage?

10. What are some benefits to having a long marriage?

QUESTIONS FOR COUPLES AT HOME

1. What dreams did we have at the beginning of our marriage that haven't been realized? Have we processed the loss of those dreams well?

2. Is there any area of our marriage where we are causing pain to each other? How can we correct that?

3. How do we typically respond to disappointment or pain in our marriage? How can we help each other respond better?

4. Are we satisfied with the amount of praise and thanksgiving we offer God in our marriage? Why or why not? How could we improve?

5. Spend time in prayer giving any loss or disappointment to God.

TO PRAY TOGETHER

Dear God,

In our marriage we have been disappointed about _____.
We acknowledge that it has been hard for us to deal with our hurt in
a godly way at times, but we want to trust you. Please bring healing
to our marriage in this area.

Lord, we also ask that we would see your goodness and favor to us.
As a couple may we remind each other of the blessings and favor you
have given to our marriage. Father, develop a greater appreciation for
your goodness to us. May we grow in thankfulness for each other and
for who you are as our Father in heaven. Today we will thank you for

_____.

In Jesus name. Amen.

SESSION NINE

Build Your Marriage
Together in Christ

AQUILA AND PRISCILLA

"Get to Know You" Question

Describe something meaningful the two of you enjoy doing together.

Overview of Aquila and Priscilla's Story

There are some couples whose names just go together. You can't have one without the other. Adam and _____? Mary and _____? David and _____? And Aquila and <u>Priscilla</u>, although the majority of times they are mentioned in the Bible, their names are reversed. We don't know why she is usually represented first, but some scholars believe it could be that she was of a higher social rank or possibly more prominent as a leader in the early church.

There's no record that they ever had children. They are only mentioned seven times in the Bible, but they were a powerhouse couple for Jesus in early Christianity. Unlike Paul or some of the other apostles, they weren't involved in full-time ministry. Together they worked as tentmakers, fabricating portable dwellings out of leather or goat's hair. This was the apostle Paul's trade as well, and perhaps that's how Paul first met them in Corinth.

Aquila was a Jew from Pontus, a region of present-day Turkey along the Black Sea. We don't know where Priscilla was from, nor do we know how they became followers of Jesus. At the time the apostle Paul met them in Corinth, they had already committed their lives to Christ. Due to Aquila's Jewish heritage they had been kicked out of Rome by the Emperor, along with all the other Jews at that time.

Everywhere Aquila and Priscilla lived, they made tents for a vocation and discipled Christians as their shared purpose in Christ. In Ephesus they heard a man named Apollos teaching powerfully about Jesus, though he had some gaps in his theology. So together, they met with him privately and taught him the things he still needed to learn. Their mutual equipping of Apollos enabled him to be more powerful for God's kingdom in reaching people for Christ.

Priscilla and Aquila also opened their homes in Ephesus and Rome for Christians to gather as a church for fellowship and worship. In his closing comments to the church in Rome, the apostle Paul says they "risked their necks" for his life, and he along with *all* the churches gave thanks to them (Romans 16:3-4). We don't know what they did that was risky, but clearly they were united in Christ and considered their relationship with him to be greater than any loss personally.

While Priscilla *may* have been more prominent than Aquila in the church, they were together in Christ. They did ministry together. They risked together. They served and traveled together.

Be thinking about how you and your spouse can grow in the unity of your relationship with Jesus. Where have you been playing it safe as a couple? What things need to be addressed or changed for you to grow deeper and more focused in your united impact for him?

SMALL GROUP DISCUSSION QUESTIONS

1. Daydream for a minute. If you and your spouse could do any ministry together, what would you do? Describe your dream.

2. Read Acts 18:1-4, Acts 18:18-19, and Acts 18:24-28. What do we know about Priscilla and Aquila? What was their relationship with Paul?

3. How did Priscilla and Aquila partner together in ministry? How do you think they grew together spiritually?

4. What are some ways that a husband and wife can grow spiritually together? Which of these do you practice regularly in your marriage?

5. In Acts 18:24 we are introduced to Apollos. Who is he? Was he a false teacher? Why do you think Priscilla and Aquila invited Apollos to their home? How do we know they were successful in their purpose?

6. Read Romans 16:3-4. What risks have you as a couple taken for Jesus? Do you think you may have been playing it too safe?

7. Why is it important for married couples to read the Bible and pray *together*, not just independently or on their own? Do you regularly read the Bible together and pray together? Why or why not?

8. What is your biggest hindrance to growing spiritually together? What are some ways you can prioritize your spiritual growth as a couple?

9. It's important as parents to train our children spiritually. As a small group, share ways that you are training (or have trained) your children to love God. What ideas worked well for you? Brainstorm some new ideas to raise your kids in a godly home.

10. Think back over the previous sessions. Take a moment to review them. What stands out as particularly impactful for you in your marriage? Share with the group.

QUESTIONS FOR COUPLES AT HOME

1. On a scale of 1-10, where would you say we are when it comes to being united in Christ? (10 is best.)

2. Where do we need to take greater risks for Jesus? What hinders us from that?

3. What are two things we could do to grow spiritually together? How will we accomplish this?

4. How can I pray for you?

5. Spend time together praying for unity and spiritual growth in your marriage.

TO PRAY TOGETHER

Dear God,

Thank you for bringing us together in marriage. We know that marriage is a covenant between you and us. Protect our marriage from the enemy who would like to destroy our unity. We recognize that you brought us together to love you, to be a witness to others by giving you glory and praise, and to encourage each other through our marriage. Strengthen us as a couple. Grow us in our knowledge of the Bible and its application to our lives. Deepen our love for you and each other. Protect our minds from false teachings and deceptive thoughts.

We ask that we will be consistent in the reading of your Word, attending a local church together, developing friendships with other Christ-followers, serving you faithfully, giving our time and financial resources to you, and praying for our marriage, our family, our friends, and others. We ask for unity in our marriage as we grow together spiritually.

In Jesus' name. Amen.